MAPPING EARTHFORMS

Valleys

Melanie Waldron

Heinemann Library
Chicago, Illinois

Designed by Richard Parker and Q2A solutions
Illustrations: Jeff Edwards
Picture Research: Hannah Taylor
Production: Duncan Gilbert

Originated by Chroma Graphics (Overseas) Pte. Ltd
Printed and Bound in China by Leo Paper Group

11 10 09 08 07
10 9 8 7 6 5 4 3 2 1

ISBNs: 978-1-4034-9607-2 (hardcover)
       978-1-4034-9617-1 (paperback)

Library of Congress Cataloging-in-Publication Data

Waldron, Melanie.
  Valleys / Melanie Waldron. -- 1st ed.
     p. cm. -- (Mapping earthforms)
  Includes bibliographical references and index.
  ISBN-13: 978-1-4034-9607-2 (library binding - hardcover)
  ISBN-10: 1-4034-9607-2 (library binding - hardcover)
  ISBN-13: 978-1-4034-9617-1 (pbk.)
  ISBN-10: 1-4034-9617-X (pbk.)
  1. Valleys--Juvenile literature. I. Title.
  GB562.W35 2007
  551.44'2--dc22
                        2006037721

Acknowledgments
The publishers would like to thank the following for permission to reproduce photographs:
Alamy Images pp. 21 (Arch White), 13 (Bill Bachman), 20 (Hemis); Corbis pp. 16 (Craig Tuttle), 18 (Darrell Gulin), 26 (Eye Ubiquitous/David Cumming), 15 (James Marshall), 7 (Keren Su), 24 (Tom Bean); FLPA/Minden Pictures/Jim Brandenburg p. 19; Getty Images pp. 4 (Digital Vision), 27 (Stone); Photolibrary pp. 5, 25 (Index Stock Imagery), 17 (Survival Anglia), 10 (T C Middleton); Rex Features pp. 11 (Sunset), 23 (The Travel Library); Science Photo Library pp. 8 (Annie Poole), 9 (CNES, 1989 Distribution SPOT Image).

Cover photograph reproduced with permission of Photolibrary/Pacific Stock.

Every effort has been made to contact copyright holders of any material reproduced in this book. Any omissions will be rectified in subsequent printings if notice is given to the publishers.

Contents

Any words appearing in the text in bold, **like this**, are explained in the Glossary. You can find the answers to Map Active questions on page 29.

What is a Valley?

Valleys are landforms that appear in many different places all over the world. They carve out **channels** between steep mountains, gentle hills, rolling countryside, and flat land. Sometimes they take water all the way from mountain peaks to the sea. Sometimes they are dry, with no water in them at all. Some valleys contain huge **glaciers**, or rivers of ice.

All valleys have land that rises on either side of them. In **river plain valleys** this land can rise gently, far away from the valley floor. These valleys can have wide, flat valley floors. In **V-shaped valleys** the land can rise very steeply, straight up from the valley floor, with no flat land in between. In **U-shaped valleys**, the bottom of the valley is a deep, wide channel and the sides are very steep.

▼ Valleys are what make mountains such as the North Cascades in Washington so dramatic. Without valleys, the land would be flat and the peaks would not rise so sharply into the sky.

▲ Valleys such as the Otz Valley in Austria can provide ideal places to set up homes and farms. Wide, flat valley floors are especially useful for this.

How are valleys formed?

Most valleys form because of **erosion**. Erosion is the wearing away of land, including rocks, soil, and the plants that grow on them. The land in many valleys is eroded by water. In high mountainous areas and in cold areas, the land can be eroded by ice. Both the water and the ice are controlled by **gravity**. Gravity pulls the ice and water downhill until it reaches the sea. A few large valleys have formed in a different way. They formed when large cracks in Earth's surface opened up, and the land in between has dropped.

Life in a valley

There are so many different valleys all over the world that life in each one is different. In mountainous areas, plants and animals have **adapted** to living on steep slopes and in cold weather. In wide, flat valleys humans have used the land to grow crops, to raise animals, and to build houses, offices, and factories. Across the world, many different plants, animals, and humans have made valleys their home.

Valleys of the World

Valleys are found all over the world, wherever water or ice has moved downhill and eroded the land on its way. In some places valleys are steep and deep, while in other places valleys have gentler slopes and are more shallow. The shape and depth of a valley depends on many things. It depends on the type of rock that the land is made of. It also depends on the amount of water or ice flowing over the land.

Canyons (also known as **gorges**) are types of valleys. They usually have very steep sides, which are often straight up and down. Canyons usually form in areas where the rock is extremely hard. This means that it cannot be easily eroded. Over time, the water flowing over the land manages to cut down into the rock, and eventually leaves behind a deep valley with **vertical** sides. The Grand Canyon in Arizona is a magnificent example of a canyon.

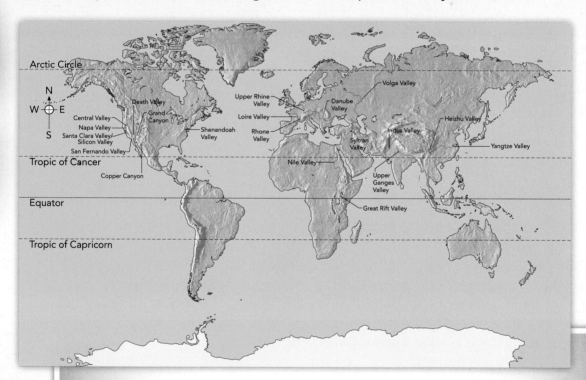

▲ This map shows some of the larger valleys of the world. However, there are many thousands of valleys, found in most countries of the world. Valleys can range in size from tiny notches in mountainsides to huge, flat-bottomed basins. Most of the valleys labeled on this map are so large that they change in character from top to bottom.

▲ Some valley settlements have very little flat land to build on. People carve out small areas of flat land into the steep valley sides. Crops can also be grown on flat **terraces** built into the hillsides.

Valleys across the world, such as the Indus Valley in Pakistan, have been home to some of the world's ancient civilizations. This is because valleys can provide many things. They provide some shelter from harsh weather, and the flat land on valley floors provides a good site for buildings. As most valleys have rivers running through them, there is a good supply of water for drinking, cooking, and growing crops. The soil on flat valley floors is often thick and **fertile**, so crops grow well. Rivers in valleys also provide excellent transport links with other settlements.

Today, valleys across the world have many different uses. Many mountain valleys, such as the Alps in Europe, are very beautiful and attract many tourists. The Nile Valley in Egypt is the only place in Egypt where crops can be grown, as the land elsewhere is too dry. Valley settlements range from small villages clinging to steep valley sides to large towns and cities on flat valley floors.

V-Shaped Valleys

In many mountainous and upland areas, the rock is hard and forms steep slopes. Rainwater or meltwater from snow and ice runs down these slopes. The water is pulled down by **gravity** and starts to collect in small streams. As these streams join together to form larger streams, the energy of the water increases.

Cutting down

Mountain streams usually contain pebbles, rocks, and boulders that have broken off the mountainsides and tumbled into the streams. The water in mountain streams must find its way around these rocks because it is being pulled downward by gravity. As the water twists and turns around these rocks, it picks up small particles from the stream bed and carries them downstream. This is known as **vertical erosion** because the water erodes down into the rock. Over time, this **downcutting** process gradually deepens the stream bed, wearing away the mountainside until a *V* shape starts to form.

Interlocking spurs

In some **V-shaped valleys**, the stream does not run in a straight line and instead flows in a zig-zag shape. This happens because water always tries to find the easiest way down the mountain. If there is an area of particularly hard rock in the way, the water will flow around it. Over time this causes the river to wind side to side. If you looked up a valley, you would see the valley sides interlocking with each other as the stream winds past the areas of harder rock. These sections of land are called **interlocking spurs**.

◀ V-shaped valleys such, as this one in the Swiss Alps, have very little flat land at the bottom. The river cuts down into the land, leaving steep sides. Sometimes rocks can fall from these steep sides and end up in the river.

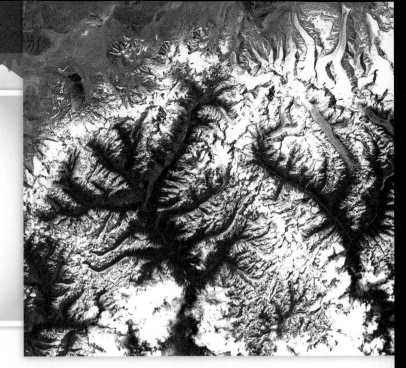

▶ Upland areas, such as this one in Bhutan, can be split by numerous small V-shaped valleys. Many of these small valleys will eventually **converge** to form bigger valleys with larger streams at the bottom.

As mountain streams begin to join together and move farther down the mountain slopes, the **gradient** of the land begins to flatten out. There, the water is not pulled downward by gravity as much. This means that the vertical erosion becomes less, and there is less downcutting. The valley shape starts to change from a steep *V* shape to a flatter, gentler *V* shape.

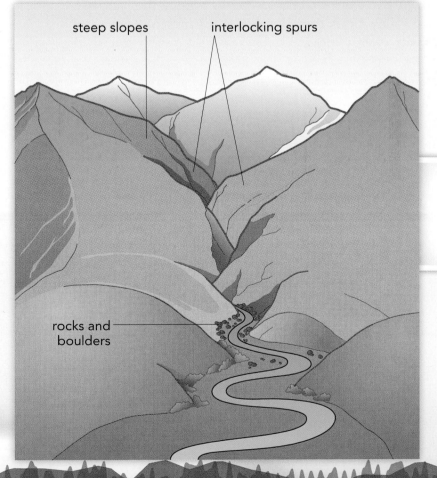

steep slopes

interlocking spurs

rocks and boulders

◀ This is a cross-section of a *V*-shaped valley.

U-Shaped Valleys

U-shaped valleys also form in mountainous and upland areas. Most of them were formed thousands of years ago during the **Ice Ages**. These were times when Earth's **climate** was very cold. The last Ice Age ended about 10,000 years ago. During the Ice Ages, huge rivers of ice called **glaciers** formed in mountainous areas and gradually moved down slopes, creating valleys. Today most of these glaciers no longer exist, so we can see the amazing landforms they left behind.

Plucking and grinding

As glaciers move downhill, they are able to erode the land at an incredible rate. This is because the ice is so hard and the glaciers are so huge. Any rock, soil, and vegetation in their path is simply pushed out of the way. Glaciers erode by plucking rocks straight from the valley floor and sides, and by grinding up large boulders as they pass over them. These huge rivers of ice simply bulldoze their way down valleys, leaving behind a wide, deep *U* shape.

Glacial features

Many valleys that have been created by glaciers show similar features:
• **Truncated spurs** — The valley sides are eroded away where the glacier passes. This leaves behind valley sides that slope down from the top, then suddenly drop straight to the valley floor.

▼ The immense power of glaciers can be seen here in the Cairngorms in Scotland, where they have carved out huge, deep *U*-shaped valleys in the landscape.

◀ *U*-shaped valleys are continuing to form today, as huge glaciers such as the Aletschgletscher glacier in Switzerland flow steadily downhill.

- **Hanging valleys** — These are created when tributary glaciers (small glaciers that join the main glacier) exist. The glaciers are smaller, so they do not erode as deep or as wide as the main glacier. The valley of the tributary glacie, therefore, is higher than the main valley. When the glaciers melt, streams flowing in the hanging valley often fall as waterfalls down to the main valley.
- **Ribbon lakes** — Where the glacier gouges out deep **channels** in the valley floor, long, thin ribbon lakes are left behind when the glacier melts. The water is held in the lake by piles of **moraine**. Moraine is the boulders, rocks, and pebbles left behind when a glacier retreats and melts.

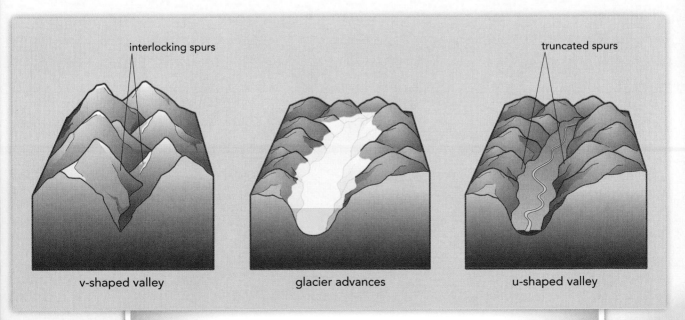

interlocking spurs

truncated spurs

v-shaped valley

glacier advances

u-shaped valley

▲ The cross-section shows how a *U*-shaped valley forms.

River Plain Valleys

Many valleys are found in lowland areas where the land is flatter and the rocks are softer. These **river plain valleys** are usually very wide, with flat valley floors and gently sloping sides. When you look at the rivers that flow through these valleys, they seem to be too small to have created such a wide valley floor. Over time, however, this is exactly what they have done.

▼ River plain valleys can be very wide. This makes them good places for settlements to grow, but there are problems with building on the flat valley floor.

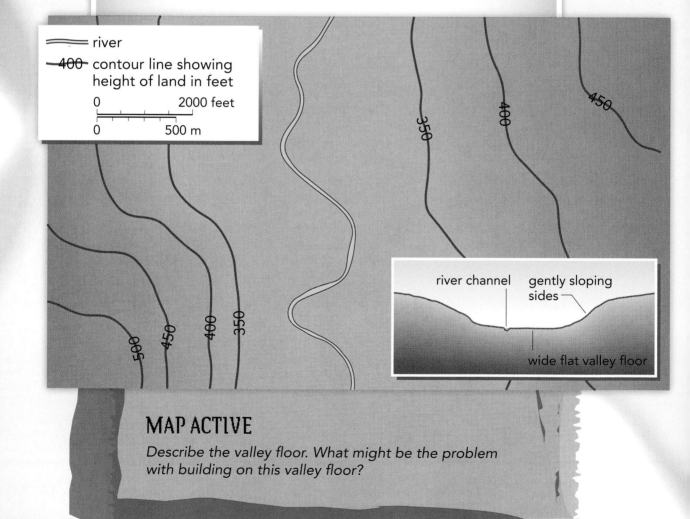

river

400 contour line showing height of land in feet

0		2000 feet

0		500 m

350
400
450

500
450
400
350

river channel   gently sloping sides

wide flat valley floor

MAP ACTIVE

Describe the valley floor. What might be the problem with building on this valley floor?

▲ Upper Murray Valley in Victoria, Australia, is an example of a river plain valley.

Lateral erosion

Because the land is flatter in these areas, **gravity** does not pull down rivers as strongly there. This means that they do not erode deep into the ground. Instead, as the river slowly **meanders** its way across the land, it tends to erode the sides of the river **channel**. Over time, this can allow the river to move side to side across the valley floor, gradually wearing away the land to form a wide, flat valley floor. This sideways erosion is called **lateral erosion**.

Useful flooding

River plain valleys often flood. This is because the rivers flowing through them are formed by lots of small streams and rivers in upland areas that join together to form one big river. This means that after heavy rainfall, the lowland river will have to cope with extra water from all the small streams and rivers. Also, as these rivers tend to create lateral erosion rather than **vertical erosion**, they are often not very deep. However, flooding is not always a bad thing!

As these rivers spill out over their banks and onto the flat valley floor, they spread out over a wide area. Any particles of **silt** or **sediment** carried by the river drop out onto the land, and over time this builds up deep and **fertile** soils on the valley floors. This makes river plain valleys good places for growing crops and grazing animals. However, the risk of flooding is always present.

Connecticut River Valley

The Connecticut River Valley in the Northeast was originally carved out by **glaciers** during the last **Ice Age**. Toward the end of the Ice Age, when the glaciers began to shrink, a lake called Lake Hitchcock filled the valley floor. During this time, layer upon layer of **sediment** formed on the valley floor at the bottom of the lake. Around 12,000 years ago, the lake started to drain, and since then the Connecticut River has run through the valley, cutting its way through the layers of sediment that line the valley floor.

Humans have been living in the Connecticut River Valley since the end of the Ice Age. Native Americans hunted caribou and the now-extinct woolly mammoth. Europeans first entered the valley in the early 1600s.

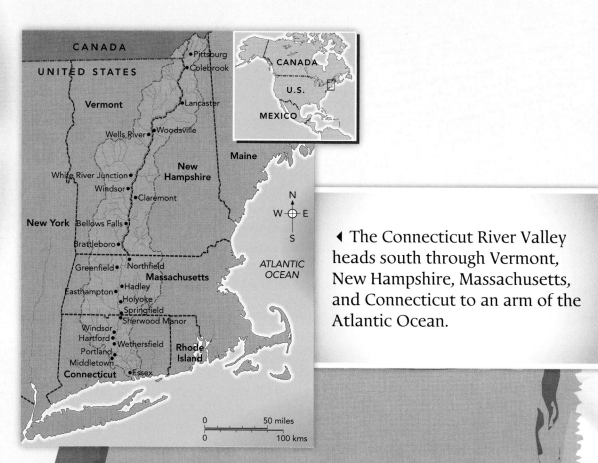

◀ The Connecticut River Valley heads south through Vermont, New Hampshire, Massachusetts, and Connecticut to an arm of the Atlantic Ocean.

MAP ACTIVE

There are many towns and cities along the length of the Connecticut River Valley. Describe any likely problems with this.

◀ The Connecticut River Valley is lined in places by beautiful trees, seen here changing color in autumn.

Plants and animals

Because the valley floor is made up of sediment such as silt, sand, and gravel, the soil of the valley floor is rich and **fertile**. This means that vegetation grows well in the valley and includes plants such as ferns, groundnuts, and the beautiful white birch. The river is full of life, including fish such as the shad. A huge variety of animals live in the valley, including beaver, rattlesnakes, bald eagles, mole salamanders, and white-tailed deer.

Pressures on the valley

The Connecticut River Valley is very beautiful. There are rolling hills, huge forests, **wetland** areas rich in wildlife, and historic villages. However, it is increasingly coming under pressure from a variety of activities.

- Mining — The sediment that forms the valley floor, including sand and gravel, is mined for use in the construction industry. This leaves huge scars in the landscape.
- Agriculture — The land is very rich, and valuable crops such as cigar tobacco are produced there. Dairy cows are also raised on the lush grasses to provide milk, cheese, and cream. More and more wetlands are being drained for farming.
- **Urbanization** — Increasing human populations mean that more and more land is required for building homes. This decreases the amount of land available for wildlife.

The good news is that the people and authorities of the Connecticut River Valley states realize the importance of the valley and its wildlife, and they are now taking steps to protect as much of the valley as possible.

Wildlife of Upland Valleys

In mountainous and upland valleys, plants and animals have **adapted** to living in a range of **climates**. In summer, valley floors can be hot and dry, while in the winter they can be cold and wet. Valley floors are more sheltered than higher up the valley sides, and the mountaintops are exposed. This means that plants and animals living there must be able to cope with strong, cold winds all year long, as well as cold temperatures.

Upland valley plants

The type of vegetation found in many upland valleys is known as **alpine** vegetation. There are only about 200 different **species** of alpine plants, including tussock grass. Most of these are slow growing, and most grow very close to the ground. This is to escape the worst of the windy conditions. There are some alpine trees, however, such as the bristlecone pine found in the mountains of the western United States. They can live for many years. Some have been found that are estimated to be 4,000 years old! All alpine plants have adapted to growing in thin, rocky soil. In some warm and sheltered valleys, beautiful wildflower meadows come to life in the summer. In valleys with lots of exposed rock, mosses and **lichens** are the only plants that grow well.

▸ Valleys in mountainous areas can burst into color in spring and summer when the temperatures rise.

▼ Animals such as marmots have adapted to living in mountainous valley areas.

Upland valley animals

Most animals living in upland valleys are **mammals** and birds. These animals are **warm-blooded**, which means that they create warmth for their bodies from the food they eat. Many of them have adapted ways of reducing heat loss from their bodies. Areas that lose heat quickly are legs, ears, and tails, so they have adapted to having short legs, ears, and tails to help keep them warm. Many also have special layers of fat on their bodies. Examples of alpine mammals include goats, llamas, and yaks. Some insects can also survive in this harsh environment, such as beetles and butterflies.

Wildlife of Lowland Valleys

Lowland valleys have much gentler **climates** than upland valleys. Of course, climates vary across the world, but lowland valleys usually have warm, dry summers and cooler, wetter winters. The soil in lowland valleys is usually deep and **fertile**, especially on the valley floors. This makes for ideal growing conditions for many different **species** of trees, grasses, and other vegetation. This lush vegetation can support a wide range of animals.

Because soil is often so fertile in wide, flat valley floors, people grow crops and raise **livestock** on them. Animals such as cows eat the rich green grass that grows there. Where the vegetation is left to grow wild, grasses, wildflowers, shrubs, and small trees will thrive. Where the land has been left for many years, large trees including oaks, ashes, and willows will grow into thick forests.

▼ **River plain valleys** usually have very fertile soil, so grasses and trees grow very well there. Here in the White Mountains National Forest in New Hampshire, the valley is dominated by beautiful mixed forest.

▲ Deer feed on grasses, nuts, corn, and tree shoots. They can swim and run quite fast in order to escape from predators.

Lowland animals

Many different species of animals can live well in lowland valleys, depending on the type of vegetation growing there. Valleys with rivers flowing through them will have different types of fish, and animals that eat the fish, such as bears. The water also contains many types of insects, such as water boatmen. Some birds live alongside rivers, such as the beautiful kingfisher. They feed on insects living on or in the river, and they also catch small fish such as stickleback. Some **mammals** live in and around rivers, including beavers, otters, and water voles.

In the grasslands and forests of lowland valleys, animals such as deer and foxes live. Deer eat a vegetarian diet that includes leaves, tree buds, and tender twig ends. Foxes eat just about anything! Their diet ranges from earthworms and beetles to blackberries and loganberries and to mice and birds.

Perhaps the largest valley-dweller is the bear. Bears live in forests in North America, Europe, and Asia. They eat a huge range of things, including berries, nuts, fruits, roots, fish, and some mammals.

Living in a Valley

Throughout history, people have settled in valleys. There have been many reasons for this. Probably the most common reason is that valleys offer shelter from high winds. Also, most valley floors have some flat land, which is easier to build on. Other benefits provided by valleys include water supplies, **fertile** land for farming, and good transportation routes.

Upland valleys and cultures

In upland valleys of the world, humans have **adapted** to living in the harsh **climates**. In the Himalayas of Nepal, people have to cope with hot temperatures in the valleys during the summer, and cold, windy conditions in winter.

One culture that has adapted well to upland valley living is the Sherpa culture. Sherpas have larger lungs than most other people. This is to cope with the oxygen levels in the air, which are lower in upland areas. The Sherpas also have more of a substance called hemoglobin in their blood, which transports oxygen around the body.

▼ Grenoble in France has grown to fill this section of the Isère Valley in the Alps. The city is unable to spread out sideways and, as a result, is quite crowded.

▲ Glencoe in Scotland is one of the most beautiful valleys in the world. It is sometimes difficult to imagine the violence that once happened here.

Modern valley life

Old towns and villages have grown into today's cities, which still benefit from valley locations. However, valleys can also restrict development. For example, the city of Grenoble in southern France cannot grow sideways because the valley walls are so steep. Instead, the city has grown in a long, thin ribbon shape up and down the Isère Valley. Another issue today's developments in valley floors face is flooding. Rivers can no longer be allowed to break their banks and spread over the valley floor because there are now houses and other buildings there. This means that flood protection measures line many rivers, changing the natural flow of the rivers and removing the natural beauty of the valleys.

Case study—The Glencoe massacre

Glencoe is a scenic valley in northwest Scotland. On February 13, 1692, a terrible massacre took place there. Members of the Campbell clan were staying with the MacDonald clan. The two clans were enemies, but there was a code of hospitality that meant you had to give shelter to any visitors, even to your enemies. Early in the morning, the Campbells woke and killed 38 MacDonalds. Even today some people find Glencoe eerie and threatening, despite its beauty.

A Way of Life—Norway

Norway is a long, thin country in the north of Europe. The north of the country lies inside the Arctic Circle, and in winter the sun barely rises here. Norway forms part of the region of Scandinavia, with Sweden, Denmark, Finland, Iceland, and the Faroe Islands making up the rest. It is a rich country, mostly because of its oil and gas deposits in the North Sea. Its population enjoys a high standard of living.

Norway has a very long coastline, and it is **indented** all along its length. This means that the sea winds in and out of long, narrow inlets called **fjords**. These fjords are at the ends of long, deep valleys that have been created by **glaciers**. Now rivers run through them to the North Sea. Most of the **interior** of the country is high, rocky, and mountainous, and so throughout history most of Norway's settlements have grown in the sheltered valleys around the coast.

▸ There are countless valleys in Norway's mountains and near the coast. Most towns are located around the coastline in these sheltered valleys.

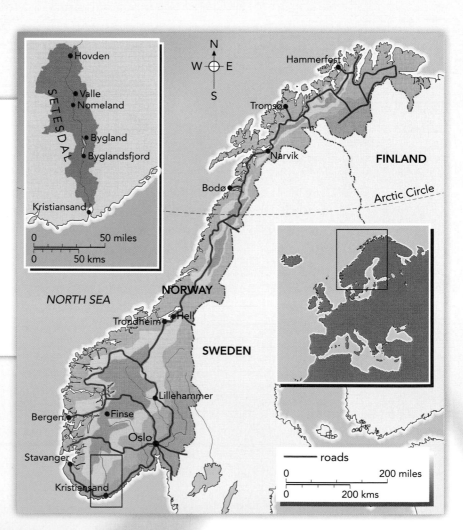

Setesdal Valley

The Setesdal Valley is a beautiful valley in the south of Norway. The Otra River runs through it, and the valley extends 140 miles (230 kilometers) south to the town of Kristiansand. The valley still contains some traditional buildings such as water mills, ancient churches, and stabburs (sheds with two floors). It was not until the 1950s that a road was built up the valley.

Traditionally, farming was the main activity for people living in the Setesdal Valley. Trade and timber were also common. Farming is still an important activity in the valley, with goats and cows as the most common **livestock**. The timber industry is also very important today, with logging and timber production providing many jobs. Modern office-based industries have also settled in the valley, especially in the larger towns such as Kristiansand.

The growing tourist industry is providing more jobs for Setesdal's population. Tourists come to go fishing, canoeing, boating, walking, skiing, and cycling. They also come to enjoy the spectacular scenery and the clean air.

▼ The Otra River is in the Setesdal Valley.

Our Changing Valleys

Nature's changes

In many upland valleys, **glaciers** continue to carve out giant *U* shapes at a very slow pace. However, in mountain ranges such as the Alps in Europe, rising global temperatures mean that many glaciers are now melting. As they melt, they retreat back up the valleys that they have created. The meltwater carries with it particles of **sediment** and rock that the glacier plucked from the ground. Over time, the wide, flat floors of these valleys fill up with this sediment and rock, changing the valley shape and the plants and animals that can live there.

Farther down these valleys, the increased meltwater makes the rivers run higher and faster, creating more **erosion** and flooding downstream.

▼ McBride Glacier in Alaska has retreated over the last few years. This is causing more meltwater to pour into valleys and erode valley floors and sides.

▲ Levees can prevent floods from damaging buildings in the flood plains of valley floors. However, areas of farmland are often allowed to flood, as the **sediment** that will be dropped by the water helps keep the soil **fertile**.

Human changes

It is in lowland **river plain valleys** where humans are having the most impact. The flat land of the valley floors is ideal for building on, and transportation routes such as roads and railways are also built here. But there are problems with development in valley floors:

- Pollution — Traffic, factories, and power stations create high levels of air pollution. In a valley, this pollution is often trapped because it does not rise high enough to clear the high ground all around. Rivers in valley bottoms can also be polluted by **urbanization** and industrialization.

- Flooding — As more land in valleys is covered with roads and buildings, the amount of land that can allow water to soak into it is decreased. When there is heavy rainfall, the rainwater simply runs off these developed surfaces and into streams and rivers, causing them to flood more quickly.

- Flood control — To deal with the issue of flooding, many rivers in valleys have been straightened and deepened. This is called canalization. It affects the wildlife living in and around the rivers, and it causes more flooding problems downstream because it simply moves the water somewhere else. Flood protection measures such as **levees** have also been built.

Looking to the Future

Valleys are found all over the world and range from small river valleys to huge, wide lowland valleys. Many valleys have already been developed and lost some of their natural beauty. However, there are still many beautiful valleys in the world. People need to work hard to make sure they remain beautiful. Controlling development is one way to do this.

Upland valleys

Upland valleys are most at risk from **climate** change. In order to prevent this, we need to try to reduce the amount of gases that we create. These gases, such as carbon dioxide and sulphur dioxide, are produced by vehicle engines and by burning coal and oil to produce electricity. If we use less electricity and more public transportation, we can help reduce the levels of these gases. Another impact on upland valleys is tourism. While activities such as skiing, mountaineering, walking, and cycling help bring money to upland areas, sometimes the environment suffers and wildlife is affected.

▶ The Danube River in Budapest, Hungary, is lined by a deep embankment to prevent flooding. In places this lessens the natural beauty of the area.

▲ Many valleys are beautiful, tranquil places that deserve to be protected from future development.

Useful flooding

While flooding is a problem in towns and cities, in valleys with few buildings flooding can actually be beneficial. All the **sediment** and **silt** carried by floodwater is dumped on the land, and this helps keep the land **fertile**. Also, allowing a river to flood in some places helps avoid flooding in other places.

Conservation in action

In many countries, communities have already taken action to protect their beautiful valleys. An example is the Valley Conservation Council in Virginia. Its aim is to "promote land use that sustains the farms, forests, open spaces, and cultural heritage of the Shenandoah Valley region of Virginia." The group recognizes that some development needs to take place to cater to the area's growing population. However, it aims to ensure that development is carried out in such a way that protects the valley's natural resources.

Valley Facts

Valleys in space

Did you know that valleys are found on the Moon and on some other planets? They have been formed in different ways from valleys on Earth and are more likely to have been created by meteorites, rock movements, or lava flows.

- The largest space valley system found so far is on Mars. It is called the Valles Marineris, and the **canyons** and valleys cover an area of 2,800 miles (4,500 kilometers) by nearly 400 miles (600 kilometers). Up to 6 miles (10 kilometers) deep in places, the valley system is around 10 times longer than the Grand Canyon.

- In the Southwest, canyons are important sites for archaeology because of the many cliff dwellings built into the canyon walls. The ancient Pueblo people built most of these.

- The deepest canyon in the world is Yarlung Tsangpo Canyon in Tibet, China. The Brahmaputra River runs through it.

- The Khumbu Valley in Nepal is one of the mountaineering world's most famous valleys. It leads up to the sides of Mount Everest, the highest mountain on Earth. Close to Mount Everest, the Khumbu Valley contains one of the most dangerous parts of the trek up the mountain. This is the Khumbu icefall, a huge glacier criss-crossed by deep gaps called crevasses. The ice moves and collapses regularly, and many climbers have lost their lives in this part of the valley.

Find Out More

Further reading

Brimner, Larry Dean. *True Books: Earth Science—Valleys and Canyons*. New York, NY: Children's Press, 2000.

Peterson, David. *True Books: Nationals Parks—Grand Canyon National Park*. New York, NY: Children's Press, 2001.

Trumbauer, Lisa. *Rookie Read-About Geography: Grand Canyon*. New York, NY: Scholastic, 2005.

Web sites

www.travelhudsonvalley.org
Explore the Hudson River Valley, New York, from its history to its environment.

www.nationalgeographic.com/grandcanyon/kids.html
Enjoy games and activities centered on the Grand Canyon.

Map Active answers

Page 12: The valley floor is flat and wide. The river runs along the valley floor, bending from side to side through the valley. The problem with building on this valley floor is that the river may flood in times of heavy rain. Also, over time the river may continue to bend side to side and may eventually run a different course through the valley floor.

Page 14: There are many towns and the cities in the Connecticut River Valley that lie close to the Connecticut River. This may cause problems in times of heavy rainfall, when the river may flood into the valley and damage buildings. Also, there may be pollution running into the river from these towns and cities.

Glossary

adapted changed to suit certain environmental conditions

alpine anything relating to high, mountainous areas

canyon very narrow, steep-sided river valley

channel passage in the ground where water collects and flows

climate rainfall, temperature, and wind that normally affect a large area over a long period of time

converge join together

downcutting gradual erosion of rock down into the ground

erosion wearing away of rocks and soil by wind, water, ice, or chemicals

fertile rich soil in which crops can grow easily

fjord long, narrow mountain valley, carved by a glacier, which reaches the coast and has been flooded by the sea

glacier huge river of ice and compressed (packed) snow that flows slowly down a mountain

gorge narrow river valley with very steep sides

gradient steepness of a slope

gravity force that causes all objects to be pulled toward Earth

hanging valley a tributary (smaller) valley that is higher than the main valley into which it flows

Ice Age period of time in Earth's history when temperatures were much lower and ice and snow covered much of Earth's surface

indented cut into

interior inside, or middle

interlocking spurs sections of sloping land separated by a winding valley that weaves in and out of the slopes

lateral erosion wearing away in a side-to-side action, instead of down into the ground

levee raised bank at the side of a river, built up to prevent the river from flooding

lichen not a true plant; a mixture of fungus and algae

livestock farm animals such as cows, sheep, and pigs

mammal animal that feeds its young with its own milk

meander large bend in a river's course

moraine the boulders, rocks, and pebbles left behind when a glacier retreats and melts

ribbon lake long, thin body of water lying in the bottom of a glaciated valley, held back by piles of glacial moraine

river plain valley wide, flat valley, usually with a small river that flows through it

sediment fine soil and gravel that is carried in water

silt fine particles of eroded rock and soil that can settle in lakes and rivers, sometimes blocking the movement of water

species one of the groups used for classifying animals

terrace step of land cut into a hillside to provide flat land for farming

truncated spur section of sloping land that has been cut away at the bottom, usually by a glacier, leaving behind a slope that drops suddenly to the valley floor

urbanization building homes, factories, offices, shops, and roads on land that was previously natural

U-shaped valley valley carved out by a glacier, leaving behind a distinctive *U* shape

vertical straight up and down

vertical erosion cutting straight down into the ground

V-shaped valley valley carved out by a river, leaving behind a distinctive *V* shape

warm blooded using energy from food to stay at a constant body temperature

wetland areas of land that are constantly wet or dotted with pools of water

Index